Raising Start-up Finance

Time-saving books that teach specific skills to busy people, focusing on what really matters; the things that make a difference – the *essentials*.

Other books in the series include:

Making Your Money Grow

Managing Your Money

Planning Your Retirement

Making a Will

Create Great Spreadsheets

Accounting for the Small Business

Making the Most of Your Time

Reducing Your Tax Bill

For full details please send for a free copy of the latest catalogue.
See back cover for address.

Raising Start-up Finance

Phil Stone

ESSENTIALS

Published in 2001 by
How To Books Ltd, 3 Newtec Place,
Magdalen Road, Oxford OX4 1RE, United Kingdom
Tel: (01865) 793806   Fax: (01865) 248780
email: info@howtobooks.co.uk
www.howtobooks.co.uk

British Library Cataloguing in Publication Data
A catalogue record for this book is available from
the British Library

Edited by Francesca Mitchell
Cover design by Shireen Nathoo Design, London
Produced for How To Books by Deer Park Productions
Designed and typeset by Shireen Nathoo Design, London
Printed and bound by Bell & Bain Ltd., Glasgow

NOTE: The material contained in this book is set out in good faith for
general guidance and no liability can be accepted for loss or expense
incurred as a result of relying in particular circumstances on statements
made in the book. The laws and regulations are complex and liable to
change, and readers should check the current position with the relevant
authorities before making personal arrangements.

ESSENTIALS *is an imprint of*
How To Books

Contents

Preface   **7**

1   Preparing Your Case   **9**
Having a clear business proposal   10
Compiling realistic forecasts   12
Working out how much you need   15
Being ready for the presentation   21

**2   The Importance of Your Own
     Contribution**   **25**
Making your own investment   26
Gaining the support of your family   30
Using your assets to raise money   32

3   What Can the Bank Offer?   **36**
Understanding how an overdraft works   38
Considering long-term funding   40
Comparing the true costs of borrowing   42
Offering security for the debt   45

4   Alternatives for the Purchase of Assets   **49**
Using hire purchase   51
Considering leasing options   53
Obtaining a commercial mortgage   57

**5   Using Business Resources to
     Gain Funding**   **61**
     Negotiating funding from your creditors   63
     Gaining funds more quickly from your
       debtors   66
     Reducing stock levels to finance cash flow   69

6   Additional Sources of Finance   **74**
     Obtaining grants to help your business   76
     Considering funding from your Local
       Authority   79
     Understanding the role of soft loans   81
     Gaining equity funding   83

Loan Repayment Tables   **87**

Useful Contacts   **91**

Preface

Gaining the right type of funding for your business is just as important as gaining funding at all. This consideration is often missed by entrepreneurs. They believe that they have the funds themselves to start the business and do not consider outside funding to be necessary. This could be a fundamental mistake.

If you invest all of your own money into the business, what can you do when things go wrong? By that stage, all of your money has been lost and no funder is going to consider your request for borrowing. If you had gained support from the outset, and left some of your capital in reserve, matters would be entirely different. At least you could do something to rescue the business.

All it needs is for your first customer to be late in paying and you are left high and dry. If you had allowed for such contingencies in your original business plan they would not be detrimental to your business.

Gain the right mix of funding from the outset and you are more likely to succeed. It is not difficult to raise funds provided you adopt the right approach. Funders are in business to lend money. Understand what they want to see and how to approach them and you will gain their support.

Phil Stone

1 Preparing Your Case

Preparation is everything. Clear and reasonable proposals are more likely to gain support.

In this chapter, four things that really matter:

~ **Having a clear business proposal**

~ **Compiling realistic forecasts**

~ **Working out how much you need**

~ **Being ready for the presentation.**

You cannot start a business overnight and neither can you expect to gain funding overnight. You need to complete your market research and analysis and have clear strategies for the future. One in five new businesses fail within five years. There are many reasons for this high rate of failure, but the most common is lack of planning.

It is essential that you plan your new business carefully. You must undertake thorough research into the market and be clear on your objectives. As part of that process you must compile a written business plan. This will set out clearly and succinctly your research, your objectives, and more importantly, your strategy.

Is this you?

I don't need a business plan. I know what I want to do and it's a waste of time to write it all down. • What's the point of doing forecasts? Getting out and making sales is more important. • I already have sufficient funds to get started, why should I even consider the expense of borrowing money?

Having a clear business proposal

The very first thing to do is visit your bank and ask them for one of their business start-up guides. This will give you advice on the things you need to think about before even starting your business. The most important of these will be to have a clear business proposal.

Essentially this will involve a written

business plan. This will contain three basic
components: *

~ Where you are now — details of your
research into the target market.

~ Where you want to be — the goals and
objectives for your business.

~ How you are going to get there — the
strategies and resources that you will
employ to succeed.

Put yourself in the shoes of the funder. Think
about the sort of questions that they may
have about your business. Make sure that
you answer those questions in your business
plan. Ask yourself the question — would I
lend money to this business based on the
information I have before me? Remember,
you too are also risking money in this
venture. Unless you can be satisfied that you
would lend your own money, you are unlikely
to gain support from others.

Share your business plan with friends. Ask
them what they think. If you have a family,
talk through the plan with your partner.

*Be absolutely
clear. Your
business plan is
your one and only
chance to impress
a potential
funder. It is the
tool that you will
use to gain
support.*

Remember, they too will be involved in your business even if only indirectly and the whole family income could revolve around your new business.

For more detailed information on writing a business plan I suggest you read *The Ultimate Business Plan*.

Compiling realistic forecasts

As part of your planning you will need to compile a minimum of two different financial forecasts:

~ Cash flow forecast

~ Operating budget

Depending on the size of your business proposition, you may also need to prepare balance sheet and profit and loss forecasts. Once again, you can utilise the help of your bank as they can supply you with blank forecasts that you can use. In some cases, the bank may provide you with free software that you can use on your computer. As an example, Nat West provide software but you also need to have Microsoft Office installed on your computer.

Cash flow forecast

As the name suggests, the cash flow forecast deals with the cash requirements that your business will need. The easiest way to start this forecast is not to include any cash injection that you propose to make. It is better to start from nothing and then establish where the total funding will come from. This aspect is considered in the next section.

Operating budget

The operating budget will look at the profitability of your business. Profit is essential to all businesses. Without profit you are gaining no return on your investment. You are spending money to stay employed rather than earning profit from which you can be paid. No business can survive on this basis.

When compiling your forecasts you must be realistic. The potential funder will need to have faith in your figures. It is very difficult to provide answers if the figures go wrong later. You need to think about a number of things that could affect your forecasts:

~ Are my sales projections accurate?

~ When will my customers pay me — cash or credit?

~ How much credit will my suppliers give me — when will I pay them?

~ What expenses will I have — how variable are they?

Throughout your forecasts you will be making assumptions. It is important that you are able to explain the reasoning behind whatever assumptions you make. You will also need to allow for contingencies. Things that could go wrong. It is better to have pessimistic forecasts rather than optimistic ones. Look at the worst-case scenario. If that does actually happen, at least you will be prepared for it.

You must appreciate that if a funder does lend money to you based on your forecasts, they will expect your financial performance to be close to what you have projected. If it is not, and you need to go back to obtain more funding, the lender may be more wary of your proposition. *

Working out how much you need

This is the critical issue for all new businesses. Unfortunately, most get it wrong and this contributes to their downfall. If you have followed my advice with your forecasts you will not have included any opening capital. Your forecast will have established how much you actually need to start and run your business for the first year. The cash flow forecast will be showing an initial negative figure. This figure should, if you are making a profit, decline in value over the period of the forecast.

Only now can you consider sources of funding and arrive at a suitable financial package for your new business. In this

* Get the forecasts right from the beginning and you stand more chance of retaining a funder's confidence.

respect you will need to look at two different aspects:

~ What do I want the money for?

~ How quickly can it be repaid?

The sample cash flow forecast shown below makes a number of assumptions regarding debtor and creditor payment times. It is not relevant to discuss them now, but you will need to make your own assumptions in this regard. The major factor is the bottom line — the bank balance. As you can see, this peaks with a funding requirement of just under £70,000 in the second month. The requirement then falls steadily over the first six months.

What you need to consider is where that funding will come from. The next factor is whether the funding should be long-term or short-term. For the moment we will assume that you have a total of £50,000 to invest in your new business.

	Month 1	Month 2	Month 3	Month 4	Month 5	Month 6
Sales						
Product 1	4,000	5,500	6,500	7,500	7,500	7,500
Product 2	2,000	3,500	5,500	5,500	6,500	6,500
Product 3	2,000	3,500	5,000	5,000	5,000	8,000
Total	8,000	12,500	17,000	18,000	19,000	22,000
Receipts						
Debtors	4,000	8,250	13,625	16,375	18,250	20,250
Owners						
Grants						
Loans						
VAT due	700	1,444	2,384	2,866	3,194	3,544
Total	4,700	9,694	16,009	19,241	21,444	23,794
Payments						
Raw Materials	2,800	4,375	5,950	6,300	6,650	7,700
Wages	3,500	3,500	3,500	3,500	3,500	3,500
Rent	1,200	1,200	1,200	1,200	1,200	1,200
Rates	200	200	200	200	200	200
Insurance	1,650			1,650		
Heat, Light, Power	2,000	450			450	
Telephone	650		350			350
Advertising	3,500	500	500	500	500	500
Stationery	465	465	465	465	465	465
Travel	200	200	200	200	200	200
Professional fees	2,500	500			500	
Repairs	100	100	100	100	100	100
Other	100	100	100	100	100	100
Capital Expenditure	40,000					
Bank charges						
Loan repayments						
Interest						
Drawings	1,500	1,500	1,500	1,500	1,500	1,500
Tax due						
VAT due	9,155	1,171	1,341	1,341	1,569	1,648
VAT payments	0			(7,139)		
Total	69,520	14,261	15,406	9,917	16,934	17,463
Balance	(64,820)	(4,567)	603	9,323	4,510	6,331
Bank balance	(64,820)	(69, 387)	(68,784)	(59,461)	(54,951)	(48,620)

Sample cash flow forecast

As you can see, the majority of the funding – £40,000 – is required for capital expenditure. This is a long-term investment in the business. The balance of the funding requirement – £30,000 – is to fund working capital. Note the substantial reduction over the six month period. This gives the following overall funding requirement:

~ Long-term funding – £40,000

~ Short-term funding – £30,000

For the moment let us concentrate on the long-term funding. Assume that the capital expenditure is to be spent in two main areas:

~ Tools and equipment – £25,000

~ Vehicles – £15,000

This could be funded in a number of different ways. It could be funded entirely from your own pocket, although that would restrict your choices later. As it is probably easier to gain funding for capital expenditure than for any other purpose, you need to take advantage of this.

The tools and equipment are going to last you, say, a minimum of three years. In the same way, the vehicles will also probably be good for three years. On this basis, funding over a three-year period is probably most appropriate. The question is: how much should you put into the package?

It would not be unreasonable to borrow half of the requirement for tools and equipment. It is also possible that grants could be available for such items. For the purposes of this exercise, let us assume 15% of expenditure. The motor vehicles could be funded, for example, by loan, hire purchase, or leasing. In most cases a deposit of 20% would be adequate.

This would create the following potential funding requirement:

~ Tools and equipment – £12,500 debt + £3,750 grant + £8,750 owner's capital = £25,000

~ Motor vehicles – £12,000 debt + £3,000 owner's capital = £15,000

At this stage, you can see that your total investment stands at £11,750, or just under 30% of the total long-term funding. This would not be unreasonable. It also leaves a number of options open. For example, bearing in mind the short-term funding of £30,000 required, even if this were to be funded entirely by you, bringing your total investment to £41,750, this would still leave a healthy £8,250 in reserve.

This is not, however, the best solution. The short-term funding requirement is extremely short-term. It would not be unreasonable to ask the bank for an overdraft of half the requirement, i.e. £15,000, for a six-month period. This would bring your total investment to £26,750 against total borrowing of £39,500 and grant funding of £3,750. This solution also leaves you with £23,250 in reserve. *

* Never consider investing all of your own funds into your business. Gain the best possible package of funding and you leave options open for later. Having funds in reserve to cover contingencies is a far better strategy.

Once you have decided the funding requirement, make sure you amend your financial forecasts to take account of these figures. Do not forget to put in suitable repayments within the expenses section of the cash flow forecast.

Being ready for the presentation

So far you have done your research, written your business plan, compiled your forecasts and decided on the right funding package. What now? First of all, check all your plans again. Make sure they stand up to criticism. Look at all the angles again and ensure that you have covered every possible eventuality. If there are any questions left unanswered, make sure you answer them. If you can show the potential funder that you have considered every question they may ask, they should be suitably impressed. *

Compare the words in the business plan to the figures in the forecasts and make sure they match. It is pointless stating in words that you are going to spend £x on capital expenditure if the forecasts reflect £y.

If the forecasts have been prepared by someone else, for example your accountant,

Cover all the points raised in this chapter and you will increase you chances of success.

make sure you understand them. The business plan and forecasts are yours and they must reflect your goals and objectives. The accountant will not be monitoring your ongoing performance, you will. You must ensure that you understand the underlying assumptions in the forecasts and be able to explain clearly and succinctly why you have made those assumptions.

~ The number of plans I have seen that have been written by two different people is astonishing. This was fine in itself if they had taken the trouble to work together. They obviously had not because invariably the wording did not match the financial information. This certainly did not inspire confidence and inevitably their request for funding was declined.

Only once you are entirely happy with your business plan and forecasts should you present them to a potential funder. *

You only get one chance to impress and you need to make sure you use it to your advantage.

It may have taken you a number of weeks to put the proposal together, so allow the funder sufficient time to properly analyse your proposition. Push them for a quick decision on granting the funding and it may well be 'no' simply because you are not giving them sufficient time to review your request.

~ The best meetings I have had regarding requests for funding did not involve any real discussions about the business plan. I was already sold on the concept and as a result the only discussions were about the terms of the borrowing.

Summary points

★ Plan your new business carefully. Make sure you have researched the market thoroughly and have clear business objectives.

★ Involve your bank from the outset. Use their business start-up guide to help you write your business plan.

★ Prepare your financial forecasts based on a

worst-case scenario. If the worst actually happens you will then be prepared for it.

★ Do not consider investing all of your own financial resources into your business. Gaining the right form of funding is extremely important.

★ Once your business plan is complete and your financial forecasts have been compiled, check them all thoroughly before sending them to a potential funder — you only get one chance so make sure you get it right first time.

2 The Importance of Your Own Contribution

Your investment in your business is your risk capital. If you won't take a risk why should anyone else?

In this chapter, three things that really matter:

~ **Making your own investment**
~ **Gaining the support of your family**
~ **Using your assets to raise money**

Without a financial contribution from you, your request for finance will fail. At the same time, even if you do have a substantial contribution your request may still fail. The size of the contribution is not always relevant. The underlying business proposition is the primary factor. Without a coherent proposal that stands a good chance of success you will not gain finance.

The potential funder will also be looking for total commitment from you. This means that you must have an adequate investment in your business. This has, in part, been explored in the previous chapter. The question of what amount is adequate cannot be satisfactorily defined. It will depend on the proposition.

Is this you?

I've got a really great business idea but I can't get anyone to finance me, even though it stands to make a lot of money. • My investment in my business is the skills and experience I have, surely that's enough? • My family life is not going to be affected by starting my business because I'll still work the same hours.

Making your own investment

Before you can even consider raising funds from external sources you must make your own investment. This investment can take two main forms:

~ Financial

~ Non-financial

Financial investment, as the name suggests, is a direct injection of cash into your business. If you are operating as a limited liability company, this could take the form of share capital or director's loan. If you operate either as a sole trader or partnership, it will be classified as owner's or partner's capital.

The decision as to which type of business to operate can be complex. There are advantages and disadvantages to operating as a sole trader, or partnership, or as a limited liability company. From the outset you need to seek professional advice on this aspect.

Non-financial investment is the introduction of assets that you may already own. For example, motor vehicles and tools and equipment. These need to be carefully valued for inclusion in your financial records. If you are introducing assets into your business in this way you are advised to seek the help of an accountant. This will ensure that your assets are correctly valued and that they comply with any Inland Revenue guidelines.

As I have outlined previously, there can be no hard and fast rules on how much capital is required. *

In this book, however, we are looking at raising finance for your new business. It is important that you understand the basic criteria used by funders — that of 'gearing'.

What is 'gearing'?

'Gearing' is the relationship between your funds in the business, the owner's capital, and borrowed money or debt. Let us assume that your new business has £5,000 capital and you are seeking £7,500 of borrowed funds. Gearing is calculated by dividing one by the other and can be expressed in one of two ways:

~ Gearing percentage — £7,500 ÷ £5,000 x 100 = 150%

~ Gearing ratio — £7,500 ÷ £5,000 = 1.5:1

* You can, of course, never have too much capital. What you do need to do is to make sure that you use it wisely.

This shows that for every £1 of capital there are debts of £1.50. Gearing of more than 100% or 1:1 is considered high. Gearing of less than 100% or 1:1 is considered low. This means that with low gearing the owner is shouldering the majority of the risk. Conversely, with high gearing, the lender is assuming more risk than the owner.

For a small business looking to raise finance for the first time any lender will probably be looking for gearing as close to 100% as possible. Having said that, there is no 'perfect' gearing ratio and each proposition is considered on its merits.

Consider the example given in Chapter 1. In this case, there was capital of £26,750 and debts of £39,500 which, under those specific circumstances, was not unreasonable. This would give gearing of close to 148% if you ignore the grant funding. If you include the grant of £3,750 which is, in effect, also being invested in the business as capital, gearing reduces to 130%. *

Some of the most extreme gearing levels occur in management buy-outs, which can often be in excess of 1000%. It is all a question of balancing the proposition with the right mix of funding.

Gaining the support of your family

Starting your own business can be very daunting and can affect your family or home life in many different ways. If you have previously been in employment you can, for example, say goodbye to the standard nine-to-five working life. You may find that your home life and your business life suddenly become less distinguishable from each other.

You must also remember that if you are giving up a job to start your own business, the regular salary or wage payments will cease. Your income will depend entirely on how successful your business becomes. This emphasises the need to have proper funding in place from the start and the importance of having something in reserve.

If you have a family you will require their strong support. Working for yourself is not an easy option and it will require hard work, with the probability of long hours. Remember that paid holidays and days off sick will be a thing of the past. Weekends will also probably be encroached upon to enable you to deal with basic administration. *

* Unless you have support from your family, you will be fighting to survive on two separate fronts, at home and at work.

Financial support

Your family or other relatives could also be a source of financial support. The more resources you have at your disposal, the better. That does not necessarily mean that they have to invest financially in your business, but they may commit to helping you should things go wrong in any way. There may also be the option of family loans. As an example, if you are starting as a limited company, your relatives may be prepared to buy some company shares. Remuneration can then be made to them by the payment of dividends when the company becomes profitable.

Sharing skills

Another way that families can help is with shared skills. If, for example, you are starting your own business and you have a partner, they may be capable of dealing with basic administration. This may leave you clear to get on and run the business.

Many small businesses start in this way. It also has the advantage of demonstrating total commitment to a potential funder. This can be important when it comes to assessment of the non-financial aspects of your business plan, i.e. the additional resources that you have at your disposal. *

Using your assets to raise money

By this stage you will have realised that without an investment in your own business you will be unable to raise finance. Many small businesses start up without adequate capital resources. This problem could have been solved quite readily with a little lateral thinking.

Looking at your lifestyle

If you are starting up your own business, your whole life will change. This means that you need to reflect upon your lifestyle. It may be that many assets that you hold now, perhaps things that have been built up over many years, could be put to better use. Let me be clear – I am not suggesting that you consider selling the family heirlooms in order

* Unless you have the total support and commitment of your family, you will stand little chance of success.

to finance your business. What I am saying is that you need to take stock and look at how your life will change. Some of the assets that you have now could be used to invest in your business.

It is an unfortunate fact that each year many people are made redundant. This can give them a number of choices, the most common of which are probably:

~ Try to find a new job.

~ Undertake training for a change of career.

~ Accept early retirement.

~ Start a new business.

All of these options will mean a possible change in the things that people value. Even with retirement packages being available from around the age of 50, it could mean a substantial drop in income. If you have managed to build up sufficient financial resources over the years this might solve the problem. If this is not the case, especially with the labour market as it presently is, this could mean that you have no option but to consider starting your own business.

You must remember that your new lifestyle will be affected drastically by the success, or otherwise, of your new business. Just by starting your business you are taking a risk. Your lifestyle will need to reflect that risk. Be in no doubt whatsoever that starting your own business and raising finance can be a traumatic experience. You need to be prepared for that trauma.

Converting assets into cash

You also need to take care if you are considering converting assets into cash. For example, let us assume that you have an endowment life policy. Many people make the mistake of surrendering such policies. This is a bad mistake, as you will never be able to realise the true value of that policy. As an alternative, you could investigate whether the insurance company would consider granting you a loan against the invested value. *

* Starting a new business will involve a cultural change in your life. Examine what is important and what could be changed. This may open up ways and means to finance your business.

By the same token, many people do not appreciate the assets that they already have which, if necessary, could be sold. For example, as children, many people collect items of little value at the time which in later years languish in a loft. Postage stamps would be a good example. It may be that 30 or 40 years on those stamps will have some value. Perhaps very little, but possibly quite a lot. The point is that they are no good to you where they are now.

Summary points

★ You must have an adequate investment in your business before you can attempt to raise finance from other sources.

★ Gain the backing of your family for your business and enlist them as much as possible to support you.

★ Evaluate your lifestyle and consider the changes that will be necessary when you start your new business.

★ Look at the assets that you have and see whether their value could perhaps be used to raise finance.

3 What Can the Bank Offer?

The majority of small business finance is raised from a bank. Use your bank for advice and guidance, they want to see you succeed.

In this chapter, four things that really matter:

~ **Understanding how an overdraft works**

~ **Considering long-term funding**

~ **Comparing the true costs of borrowing**

~ **Offering security for the debt**

Your bank should be the first port of call when you are looking for start-up finance. Banks operate a wide variety of special lending schemes for the start-up business. In some cases, this will also be combined with 'free' banking for an initial term, usually ranging from 12 to 18 months.

Quite apart from the financial side, your bank can also offer advice and guidance on a wide range of business concerns. These can include insurance and pension advice, through to help with taxation and other such legalities of running a business.

In most cases the business advice is offered free of charge so you should make the most of it. Banks want their business customers to succeed and you should really treat them as a partner. Talk to your bank on a regular basis and keep them informed. If for any reason your business is running into problems then seek their help at an early stage. Do not leave it so late that nothing can be done.

Is this you?

I just need an overdraft for all my funding, it keeps things simpler that way. • I don't want to borrow long-term, I should make enough in the short-term to pay off all the funding. • I don't understand why the bank is charging me twice for the same finance, are they overcharging me? • I can't offer any security, will that stop me raising money?

Understanding how an overdraft works

An overdraft is there to provide short-term working capital. Remember those key words – short-term. Overdrafts are available effectively to bridge the gap between money that is due from your customers and money that you need to pay to your suppliers. An overdraft should never be used to fund the purchase of assets unless full repayment is to be made in the short-term.

Unfortunately this critical rule is often ignored by business owners. It is vitally important that you obtain the right type of funding for your business.

~ Long-term funding for long-term investments such as the purchase of fixed assets.

~ Short-term funding for short-term requirements such as money due from debtors.

A bank overdraft works in a very simple way. An overall limit on the overdraft amount on your account is agreed between you and the bank. You are then free to draw money up to that amount, which is then repaid when you receive funds from your customers. In banking terms it is defined as an 'in and out' facility. Funds flow in and out on a regular basis to fund your working capital requirement.

Working capital

Working capital within a business is the amount of money that is held in short-term assets such as debtors and stock against the amount owed to short-term liabilities such as trade creditors. In an ideal situation, your account should swing on a regular basis from being overdrawn to being back in credit. This would mean that your short-term assets are being quickly converted into cash which is paid into the account.

This demonstrates the requirement to keep tight control of your working capital. You must always have sufficient funds to meet your liabilities as they fall due. The overdraft is there to help you in this respect but you must also retain tight control over the facility. It is essential that you do not exceed the overdraft limit without the bank's permission. Quite apart from the penalty interest that will be imposed, in some cases equating to over 30% per annum, the bank may refuse to pay cheques or other items such as direct debits.

Once this happens you have effectively lost control. No longer are you able to use the overdraft freely to pay your creditors. It is now the bank that is deciding what will be paid. You can be sure that their interest and charges will come out first. *

Considering long-term funding

* An overdraft is a primary source of finance for all businesses. Just like the other parts of your business you need to maintain tight control over how it is used.

In plain and simple terms, long-term finance is provided by a bank in the form of a loan. The name of the loan may differ between the banks but it will take one of two forms:

~ Fixed rate loan

~ Variable rate loan

A fixed rate loan means that the interest rate is fixed when the loan is granted and remains the same throughout the term of the loan. A variable rate loan is where the interest is linked either to the base lending rate or other 'managed' rate that the bank may have.

The simple difference between the two is that the repayments for a fixed rate loan will remain the same, whereas the variable rate loan repayments may increase or decrease. This means that in budgeting terms the fixed rate loan can offer an advantage. At least you know exactly how much you will repay each month. *

Fixed or variable rate?

Choosing between a fixed rate loan and a variable rate loan can be difficult. For obvious reasons it is unwise to lock yourself into a high interest loan. By the same token, when rates are low it can be unwise to take a variable rate loan. The decision rests on which way you think interest rates are going to move.

Whichever you choose, the loan will

* I have often been asked whether a fixed or variable loan would be better. My answer is simple – 'who'll win the Grand National next year?'.

generally be for a minimum of £1000, with some schemes having a maximum amount that can be borrowed and other schemes being unlimited. Repayment terms will depend upon the purpose of the loan. For example, a loan to purchase a vehicle will probably be repayable over three to five years.

Loans for the purchase of substantial fixed assets, for example land and buildings, could be available on repayment terms of up to 20 or 30 years. It is essential that you link the repayment terms to the potential life of the asset that you are purchasing. You will not, for example, be able to gain finance to purchase computer equipment if you offer to repay the loan over 20 years.

Comparing the true costs of borrowing

When you borrow money from a bank you can expect to pay a cost. This cost will come in two ways:

~ interest charges

~ arrangement fees.

We have already looked at the two different kinds of interest rate i.e. fixed rate or variable rate. These can apply on both an overdraft and a loan.

Interest is normally calculated on a daily basis. In the case of an overdraft this means that you are only paying interest when the account is actually overdrawn. Depending on your bank, the interest is then charged to the account on a monthly or quarterly basis. What this means, of course, is that if the account is overdrawn, or not sufficiently in credit in order to pay the interest, you will then pay interest upon the interest. This will affect the Annual Percentage Rate or APR that the bank will have quoted upon granting the borrowing.

Before we look at the APR concept you need to understand the imposition of arrangement fees. When the bank grants the overdraft or loan facility they will charge an arrangement fee to 'set up' the facility. In some cases this is charged on a sliding scale and in others it is calculated as a straight percentage of the total amount borrowed, say one or two per cent.

This means that if your bank agrees a loan account with a fixed interest rate of 10% and an arrangement fee of 2% you are actually paying 12%. In the case of a one-year loan this would also equate to the APR. For a loan repayable over five years, however, the APR would reduce to 10.4% because the arrangement fee is a one-off payment. This means that the cost is also spread out over the five-year term.

The important point to remember is that interest rates and arrangement fees are not always set in stone. The bank will have guidelines as to what should be charged but they are negotiable. They will also vary from bank to bank.*

Remember the bank will price the cost based on their assessment of risk. The higher the perceived risk, the higher the cost of borrowing.

Now that competition between banks and other finance providers has become so intense you should not accept the first offer. You will be trying to achieve value for money and cost efficiency within your business and you should treat the provision of finance in the same way. What you should avoid doing is playing one funder off against another. Once the bank has discussed your proposition with you and agreed an interest rate and arrangement fee, it is unlikely that they will renegotiate. *

Offering security for the debt

Depending upon the amount that you are looking to borrow, you may be asked for security. This can take the form of intangible or tangible security. Intangible security usually takes the form of a guarantee by a third party to pay your debt should you default. It may be that the bank will also require some form of tangible security to back up this guarantee. Tangible security involves a charge over assets that you may own, for example:

~ your house
~ an endowment life policy
~ stocks and shares.

* In my experience, some customers tried to bluff, stating that they had received a better offer elsewhere. My advice to them was always that they should take it.

If the bank does ask you for security and you are unwilling to provide it, despite having it available, you will need to give some very good reasons. The bank will be willing to take a risk to a certain extent, but the business is yours and you should be willing to support it. Remember the importance of commitment.

If you intend to trade as a limited company there is one other form of security that the bank may require. This is a mortgage debenture which effectively charges all of the company's assets to the bank. These will include land and buildings, stock and debtors. Of further importance to the bank is that the debenture will give them additional rights under the various Insolvency Acts, including the ability to appoint a receiver. *

* The advantages of granting security to the bank include the lower cost of borrowing. Disadvantages include the stark fact that if your business fails you will also lose your assets.

Small Firms Loan Guarantee Scheme

Even if you do not have any tangible security to offer there are other options. We have already looked at the prospect of family support and the possibility of them offering security for your debt. A further option open to the bank is the use of the Small Firms Loan Guarantee Scheme or SFLGS.

The SFLGS is a joint venture between the Department of Trade and Industry and the major high-street banks. It is available to businesses with viable business propositions but a lack of security or business track record, or both. Under the scheme the government provides a guarantee for a percentage of the total debt ranging from 70% to 85% depending on location. In return for this support a premium is paid to the government of between 1% and 2.5% per annum on the amount guaranteed. Various terms and conditions apply to the scheme and you should approach your bank for full details.

If you are able to offer security for the borrowing this should affect the perceived risk by the bank. This will also affect the interest rate to be charged. It is difficult to give precise advice on the reduction that you can expect but it should be at least 1.5% per annum.

Summary points

★ Match the type of finance to the purpose – long-term finance for long-term investment and short-term finance for short-term working capital.

★ Understand the difference between variable rate and fixed rate interest. Seek advice if you are unsure what is best for you.

★ Remember, interest rates and fees are negotiable. Make sure you get the best deal by shopping around.

★ Consider a request for security carefully. You have to match the bank's needs against those of your family.

4 Alternatives for the Purchase of Assets

When purchasing fixed assets there are alternatives to bank funding. Some of them offer a number of benefits over a conventional loan.

In this chapter, three things that really matter:

~ **Using hire purchase**

~ **Considering leasing options**

~ **Gaining a commercial mortgage**

In Chapter 1 we looked at the importance of gaining the right mix of funding. When purchasing fixed assets your options are greatly increased. There are a number of finance companies in the funding market that specialise in asset finance. In many ways, this sort of finance is easier to obtain than bank funding. This is because the asset that you are purchasing can effectively be used as security for the debt.

This can be both an advantage and a disadvantage. If you are winding up your business on a voluntary basis it gives you the option of returning the item as being no longer required. If, on the other hand, you are experiencing financial difficulty, the removal of the asset could bring about the downfall of your business.

As a prime example, consider a new start-up sole trader in business as a taxi driver. Funding the vehicle on hire purchase or leasing would probably be one option. Stop making the payments, however, and the prime asset of the business, absolutely essential to keep the business running, could be repossessed. This would inevitably lead to total failure of the business.

Is this you?

Hire purchase is the cheapest option, I can easily get one of those interest free deals. • Lease purchase is just the same as leasing, isn't it? • Leasing is no good to me, I'll never own the asset. • Why should I even think about using a building society, they only lend to people who want to buy a house.

Using hire purchase

Hire purchase can be a very easy financing option. It is also sometimes referred to as lease purchase although it is not the same as leasing. You only have to walk down your local high street to see the range of hire purchase schemes that are available, some more expensive than others. Hire purchase is an agreement to buy an asset, for example, a motor vehicle or computer equipment, with defined repayments over an agreed term. Depending upon the agreement, ownership of the asset may, or may not, pass to you immediately. Some agreements, for obvious reasons, do not allow ownership until all instalments have been paid.

In accounting terms, however, the asset is treated as yours and as such it will appear in your balance sheet. This can mean that capital allowances and the interest portion of the repayment are available to offset taxation. You will need to seek specialist advice on this aspect from your accountant. *

The disadvantages of hire purchase are the same as if you bought the asset outright. If it breaks down, unless it is under guarantee, you will be responsible for the repairs.

~ If, for example, you buy a motor vehicle on hire purchase, you are responsible for the costs of maintenance.

Breaking the agreement by returning the asset early voluntarily can also involve penalties. The hire purchase agreement is for a defined term and the finance company will price the cost of repayments based on the whole term. Hire purchase can sometimes be cheaper than traditional bank finance. This is often the case where the manufacturer of the product also provides the finance to make a purchase. Hire purchase can also be more expensive.

~ You need to check and compare the APR carefully before you sign the agreement.

Hire purchase agreements are usually quite flexible, offering either fixed or variable rates and repayment terms from 12 months to seven years. As with all other types of finance, the repayment term should be linked to the life of the asset.

This is a very important aspect. Sometimes the ease with which the finance can be gained is not necessarily in your favour. As an example, some of the high street stores offer what seem to be very good financing deals with delayed repayments, sometimes for 12 months. If you look carefully at the agreement, however, you might find that the actual APR equates to around 30% per annum. This is definitely not a good arrangement for you to sign.

Considering leasing options

Leasing is an extremely flexible form of funding. A lease is negotiated with the lessor who acquires the asset that has been chosen by the lessee. Assets that can be leased are wide and varied. Photocopiers, computer systems, office furniture, motor vehicles, machine tools and heavy plant and equipment are all examples.

Leasing should be distinguished from hiring. Hiring requires the user to select an item from stock already held by the hirer.

Leasing enables the lessee to select any item from any manufacturer or supplier. The choice is therefore unlimited. The leasing agreement will therefore be tailor-made for the actual asset involved.

There are three types of lease:

~ Finance lease

~ Operating lease

~ Contract hire

With a **finance lease**, the lessor pays for the asset and becomes the owner. The lessee then pays a rental which covers the capital cost of the asset, together with interest and service charges. The purpose of this type of lease is solely to provide finance to the lessee on the security of the asset. The lessee is responsible for all maintenance and insurance.

* Operating leases enable the lessee to avoid some of the risks of ownership, for example obsolescence.

Operating leases are mainly undertaken by manufacturers of products that tend to be highly specialised or technical. The lease usually provides that the lessor is responsible for servicing, maintenance and updating of the equipment. *

Contract hire is similar to an operating lease. One of the most common uses of contract hire is to finance a fleet of motor vehicles. In this case, the lessor takes responsibility for the regular maintenance and servicing of the vehicles. The lessee merely has to consider the day-to-day fuel costs.

Leasing provides a number of advantages over other forms of finance:

~ The lessor retains ownership of the asset and, using the asset as full security, a more competitive finance cost may be available.

~ The lease is for a fixed term and, whilst the leasing payments are being made by the lessee, the facility cannot be withdrawn unlike bank facilities which are usually repayable on demand.

~ Apart from an initial advance monthly or quarterly payment, leasing does not involve any capital outlay.

~ The lease can be flexible and in some cases the rental payments can be adjusted to take account of seasonal variations in trade.

~ The income generated by using the asset in the business should make the costs of leasing self-financing.

~ There may be tax advantages in that the whole costs of leasing can usually be offset against taxable income.

There are also disadvantages to leasing:

~ As a start-up business it can be very difficult to obtain lease finance.

~ Leased assets cannot be used as security for any other type of funding – the asset is not yours.

~ There may be restrictions on the use of the leased asset and the lessor may insist on approving your insurance arrangements.

~ Because the asset is not yours, you are not entitled to any residual value in the asset after it reaches the end of its working life.

~ There is no entitlement to claim capital allowances for taxation purposes.

Taxation issues can play a large part in the decision whether or not to use leasing. You need to examine the financial, and indeed, the non-financial factors, before you make any decision. Seek the advice of an accountant or a tax specialist to define the effects that lease finance options will have on your business.

Obtaining a commercial mortgage

With the traditional differences between banks and building societies being eroded by a competitive market, more and more financing options are available. This is even more evident now that some of the building societies have lost their mutuality and effectively converted to banks.

The advantage of a commercial mortgage over a bank loan for the same purpose is that the building society will often consider granting a greater percentage of the overall cost.

Among these is the long-term lending by building societies to commercial customers. Commercial mortgages are, in effect, the same as mortgages available to personal customers. They are, therefore, only available if you are considering the purchase of premises. *

Traditionally a bank will offer anything between 45% and 70% of the total cost of the property. In addition, the value that the bank places on the property may be based on a forced sale basis rather than an open market valuation. In simple terms, the differences between the two are:

~ Forced sale valuation – the price that the bank expects to achieve after all costs of sale and based on the principle that the property will be offered at a price to achieve a sale in the short-term.

~ Open market valuation – the price that could be achieved in the market without undue time pressure on the sale being made. It is also calculated before the costs of the sale are deducted.

Building societies, on the other hand, are usually much more flexible. They will generally lend between 60% and 90% of the open market value although in some cases they are prepared to finance 100% of the total cost of the property. Each proposition is taken on its merits. *

The repayments on a commercial mortgage can also sometimes be more flexible than for a bank loan. They can include repayment of the capital and interest on a monthly, quarterly or even annual basis.

The interest rate charged on a commercial mortgage can also be substantially lower than that charged by a bank. In some cases you could be able to negotiate an interest rate as low as 1% over base rate. In other cases the rate could be linked to the London Inter Bank Offer Rate (LIBOR), which can also be cheaper. You will, however, need to check the terms of the mortgage as to when the interest is actually charged to the loan. This can affect the APR which may in true terms be substantially more than the interest rate quoted.

A further example of the flexibility of a commercial mortgage is where repayment of the capital sum is deferred until the end of the loan, and interest only is repayable in the meantime. These are referred to as bullet repayment terms, and the loan can be repaid at the end of the term by a variety of means. These can include sale of the property, repayment from pension or life assurance proceeds, or any other secure method acceptable to the lender.

Summary points

★ Purchasing an asset gives you a number of alternative sources of finance – take time to check all of your available options.

★ Make sure that you always read all the terms and conditions of any agreement before you sign it – look for any penalty clauses.

★ Check carefully the Annual Percentage Rate (APR) that you are being charged – it can differ substantially from the interest rate quoted.

5 Using Business Resources to Gain Funding

Keeping tight control of your working capital can speed up the flow of cash into your business. Faster cash flow reduces the requirement for borrowed funds.

In this chapter, three things that really matter:

~ **Negotiating funding from your creditors**
~ **Gaining funds more quickly from your debtors**
~ **Reducing stock levels to finance cash flow**

When you establish your business you need to give a great deal of thought to your working capital requirement. Working capital is the amount you have invested in your business in terms of stock and debtors and the amount that others have invested on a short-term basis, i.e. your creditors.

You need to be aware of the implications

upon cash flow if your debtors fail to pay on time, or if you hold too much stock. Both of these tie up more cash than necessary, which could impact upon your ability to pay your debtors. In some cases this is a primary reason for business failure.

It is, therefore, important that you obtain the right balance from the outset. Remember, you can sell all of your stock at a paper profit but until you receive the cash it is not an actual profit. And until you can actually pay for the stock you have sold you are unlikely to be able to buy any more.

Is this you?

I won't be able to obtain credit, I haven't got any track record yet to enable a reference to be obtained. • I don't intend to allow any of my potential customers any credit, I can't afford to. • What difference does it make how much stock I hold or when I place any new orders? The supplier still delivers within 48 hours.

Negotiating funding from your creditors

Many start-up businesses do not consider that they will be able to gain any credit from their suppliers. This is not always the case. Trade credit, as it is known, can be available but it will depend on the circumstances. If, for example, you are starting your business at an early age having just left school or university then yes, you may have problems obtaining credit.

If, on the other hand, you have been employed for many years in the same industry that you are now starting your own business in, you may find that obtaining trade credit is not difficult. You have an established track record in the industry and probably already know the suppliers with whom you will be dealing.

~ The essential point is that you must research what is available. In other words, before you even start your business you must establish how much credit you can obtain and how long you will be given to pay. You cannot, for example, draw up any meaningful cash flow forecasts unless you assume from the outset that no credit will be available.

It can also take time to negotiate trade credit. In most cases, some form of reference will be required, probably from your bank. All banks have different philosophies when it comes to giving a reference on their customers and you will need to check the exact position with your own bank.

Keep to the terms of trade

Having gained agreement to a credit account it is extremely important that you do not abuse that facility. It can be withdrawn just as easily as it was granted and this could place severe pressure on cash flow. Always adhere to the agreed terms of the credit and make payment promptly when it is required.

~ Failure to pay on time could also render you liable to penalties.

Legislation was introduced in 1998 to allow,

under certain circumstances, for interest to be charged on outstanding invoices at the rate of 8% above Bank of England base rate. This could be a substantial amount and is therefore something that you should avoid at all cost. If, of course, your creditors start to charge you on this basis it is also likely that they will have already withdrawn your credit facility.

Using personal credit cards

Another aspect of gaining credit that most business owners ignore is the fact that personal credit cards can also, at least initially, be used for this purpose. Most credit cards allow for up to 56 days, interest-free credit provided the outstanding balance is settled in full. There is absolutely nothing to stop you using this facility for your business, although you will need to keep a careful track of the relevant records.

Do not be put off by an initial refusal, try another supplier and you may get a different answer.

Trade credit is not something that is only available to established businesses. In these times of intense competition, suppliers need to be flexible in how they make their sales. *

Gaining funds more quickly from your debtors

As you will have gathered from the previous section, whilst it may not be your initial intention to provide credit to your own customers, you may have little choice. It is important, therefore, that from the outset you realise the implications upon the funding for your business. You will be providing a loan to your customers to purchase your goods or services, such a loan to be paid at some defined time in the future.

As a consequence, it is vital that you set out clearly defined terms of trade. You also need to be sure that when you grant credit to someone you know that they will have the means to pay you. You should never be afraid of refusing credit if you are in any doubt. You may lose the sale but it is better to lose the profit element on this sale than the whole amount of the sale itself by way of bad debt. *

* You have not completed the sale until you are actually paid. All you have done is taken a gamble — consider the odds carefully before you place your bet.

When you start your business it is unlikely that you will be able to take advantage of the two main ways in which you can gain funding based on your outstanding debtors. These are:

~ factoring

~ invoice discounting.

Under normal circumstances these are only available to businesses who have a turnover exceeding £250,000 and £1 million per annum respectively. If, however, you do envisage such a turnover it is important that you understand the differences between the two.

Factoring your debts means that you can obtain an immediate advance against your outstanding debtors. This usually equates to a maximum of 80% of approved invoices. In this case, 'approved' means that the customers have been approved as debtors by the factoring company. The factor also assumes control of your sales ledger, issuing statements and reminders on a set basis.

The advantages of factoring are:

~ It improves cash flow with a faster collection of trade debts.

~ It removes the need to chase unpaid invoices.

~ It is a simple process and insurance against bad debts may be available.

The disadvantages of factoring are:

~ Your customers know that you are using the factor – in some cases this does have a stigma attached to it.

~ It can prove costly in overall terms.

~ Once you have taken out a factoring arrangement it can be difficult to extricate yourself from it.

Invoice discounting operates on broadly the same principles as factoring but with two main differences:

~ Control of the sales ledger is retained by you and you will therefore need to control the debtors and chase for late payment yourself.

~ Because you retain control, the existence of the invoice discounting arrangement is not evident to your customers – it is entirely confidential.

Because the principles are broadly the same in each case, both factoring and invoice discounting share the same advantages and disadvantages. The only difference is the perception of your customers when, rather than dealing with you concerning their invoices, they deal with the factor.

Reducing stock levels to finance cash flow

You may consider it strange that in a book about raising finance there is a section on stock included. Stock is, however, a very important consideration when you are considering finance. Holding too little stock could mean that you lose sales, but holding too much stock means that you have less cash available for other purposes. This means that you have to raise unnecessary finance which then costs you more money in interest.

~ Controlling your stock levels is, therefore, an important part of your financing.

When you establish your business, you may consider that initially you are going to require say £10,000 of stock. In itself, that will not affect your financing decisions. Provided your estimate is correct, you will actually require that amount of stock. The important question comes when you sell some of that stock and then need to replace it. How much more stock do you need and when should you order it?

Consider discounts carefully

Some businesses make the mistake of ordering in bulk in order to obtain discounts. This means that at any one time they probably have more stock than they can sell within a reasonable time. The effect of the discount is subsequently eroded because more cash than necessary is being used to finance those stock levels. If you are borrowing money for such purposes, for example, by way of bank overdraft, the interest is probably costing you more than you gain from the discount.

If, on the other hand, you ignore the offer of discounts and only purchase the stock that you can actually sell within a reasonable time, you reduce the cash requirement, and consequently the interest paid on the overdraft. In real terms this would probably mean that you are actually better off in terms of profit.

Say, for example, you sell a certain quantity of goods each day and your supplier can deliver replacement stock every other day. Theoretically, you could reduce your stock levels down to just two days' worth of sales. This would, however, be a somewhat drastic approach, as you are then relying on the supplier to deliver on time. If something happens to the delivery which delays your supplies, you could find that you have totally run out of stock.

Realistically, however, by building a contingency level into the stock requirement, you could perhaps manage by holding perhaps seven days' supply. This would mean that on the second day your shelves will be depleted but if the delivery arrives as planned this will be short-lived. If the delivery does not arrive for any reason you still have sufficient stock to trade for a further five days. This technique, referred to as 'just in time', was pioneered in Japan and is now used extensively throughout industry. *

Summary points

★ Obtaining trade credit is not impossible for a start-up business – there are likely to be many sources for your supplies, so shop around.

★ Never abuse your credit facilities – always pay your debts on time and you will establish a good track record for your business.

★ Do not forget that you can use personal credit cards to obtain interest-free credit – just make sure you keep accurate records.

There is little point in you holding a month's worth of stock when fresh deliveries can be made each week. Monitor your stock carefully and you will find that your funding requirement should be reduced.

★ Keep tight control of your debtors and make sure they pay you when they are supposed to.

★ If you are thinking of factoring or invoice discounting, consider carefully what this will mean – both can be difficult to ever repay and can be expensive.

★ Examine your stock levels on a regular basis – cash tied up in stock cannot be used for other purposes.

6 Additional Sources of Finance

Always find out what help you can get before you start. Once you have established your business it may be too late and you will miss out.

In this chapter, four things that really matter:

~ **Obtaining grants to help your business**

~ **Considering funding from your Local Authority**

~ **Understanding the role of soft loans**

~ **Gaining equity funding**

The overriding principle for obtaining grants and other forms of financial assistance is that you must make your application and have the assistance agreed before you start your business. Unfortunately, a lot of businesses miss out because they do not follow this simple rule.

There is a substantial amount of help available to new businesses in both a financial and non-financial form. It is absolutely essential that you research the position thoroughly. Some grants are reliant upon either jobs being created or investment in new plant and machinery. Others have no restrictions whatsoever and are available purely by making a simple application.

It would be impossible to cover all the forms of assistance available throughout the United Kingdom and it is up to you to find out what is available in your locality. What I can do is outline some of the types of assistance that are available to businesses in my own location, the North East of England.

Is this you?

I'm not creating any jobs so I won't be eligible for anything, will I? • I can't be bothered to apply, the forms are too complicated. • How can the Local Authority help? They don't offer anything. • I don't want anyone else having a stake in my business, I want total control.

Obtaining grants to help your business

Grants can come from a wide variety of sources, but in this section we will concentrate on the assistance provided by central government through the Department of Trade and Industry (Dti) and the Small Business Service.

The Small Business Service was established to help businesses and to represent their interests across government. It works closely with the network of Business Links in England, Business Shops in Scotland, Business Connect in Wales, and EDnet in Northern Ireland. These centres should be your first port of call if you are looking to start a business. Quite apart from the advice and guidance that they offer, they can also provide financial and non-financial grants to your business.

Financial grants from these business support organisations have, however, been substantially reduced in recent years and are only generally available in small amounts, somewhere between £100 to £250. The main provision of assistance comes in a non-financial form. Examples include help with:

~ Design and production of business cards and stationery.

~ Advice on putting together your business plan.

~ Guidance on market research and strategy for your proposed business.

Some of these take the form of training courses and others, such as design work, are undertaken by experienced professionals employed on a consultancy basis. In most cases, all of this support is offered free of charge.

Support is also available through these organisations on a subsidised basis where accredited consultants are employed to assist you and their fee is only partly payable by you. As an example, in Sunderland a 50% grant of up to £2,000 is available towards the costs of employing a professional to design your website. However, the support that will be available does vary widely and you must approach your local advice centre yourself.

Through the Dti, the government offers a number of schemes which can provide assistance in terms of either grants or awards. The main two grant schemes are:

~ Regional Selective Assistance (RSA)

~ Regional Enterprise Grant (REG)

Another example is the SMART scheme, which provides grants to review, research, or develop innovative new technology. All of these are subject to extremely rigid criteria and it has to be said that the application forms can be complicated. Within your local advice centre, however, there should be a person that can offer you advice and guidance in this respect.

The support available through the Dti is subject to constant review and change and you will need to check the current situation. The critical point to remember is that under normal circumstances, no expenditure must be incurred on the project related to the application before the grant is agreed.

Considering funding from your Local Authority

Most Local Authorities offer a range of incentives and grants for businesses to create jobs in their area. Some new businesses overlook this source of funding on the basis that they are creating no new jobs. This is factually incorrect. If you are starting your own business you are, at the very least, creating a new job for yourself.

You should contact the Economic Development Office within your Local Authority to find out what you may be eligible for, because there will be some diversity across the UK. To give you some specific examples, however, the following schemes are available from the City of Sunderland Council:

~ Rent relief grants – available for between 25% and 50% of the rent payable for the first year of a new lease.

~ Basic services grants – a 50% grant is available for the provision of new and essential services including electricity, gas or drainage work.

~ Interest relief grant – amounting to 5% per annum for up to two years of the value of loans used to purchase machinery or building for industrial use.

~ Removal grants – available to cover up to 50% of eligible costs incurred to move to industrial premises in the city.

~ Trainee employment grants – grants are awarded to cover 75% of wages of new trainees in the first year and 25% in the second year.

~ Exhibition grants – to cover 50% of the costs of exhibiting at a recognised trade exhibition outside the North East up to a maximum of £5,000.

Once the allocated amount has been expended the scheme will be suspended by the Local Authority and reviewed in the next financial year.

For obvious reasons, all of these grants have eligibility criteria, in addition to which they are entirely discretionary. This effectively means that even if you do qualify you may still not receive the funding because in simple terms the Council may not have any money left for the scheme. *

Understanding the role of soft loans

Soft loans are loans that are available on generous terms and at lower interest rates than would be charged commercially. In general terms, they are provided through local Enterprise Agencies and are available where conventional funding, for example through a bank, cannot be obtained for any reason.

Enterprise Agencies are not-for-profit organisations which provide a wide variety of services to small businesses on a localised basis. The loan funds that they operate will be available on various terms and conditions, and, in some circumstances, they are only available to people within a certain age band.

There are also many organisations that provide soft loans, the funding for which is provided by large corporations. One example of such a fund is the loan fund operated through Northern Enterprise in Newcastle-upon-Tyne which is sponsored by the

Northern Rock. A further scheme, specifically designed for young entrepreneurs, is operated by the Prince's Youth Business Trust. In a similar manner, the Royal British Legion operates a fund which is only available to ex-servicemen or women.

In some circumstances, the provision of a soft loan can actually lead to further conventional funding being raised. The reason for this is that most soft loan fund managers take a personal interest in the businesses in which they invest and accordingly they provide a high level of support and advice. This involvement can give confidence to the traditional funders, e.g. bank managers, who know that a strict degree of control will be exercised. *

This phenomenon is known as 'leverage'. The soft loan levers further funding and reduces the risks for both funders.

In some cases, there are actually informal agreements between the managers who administer the soft loans funds and the high-street banks. This works on the basis that the bank will match the amount of the loan that is made by the soft loan provider, usually up to an agreed maximum, in order that total funding for a project can be achieved on a shared basis.

Gaining equity funding

Most small businesses avoid equity at all costs on the basis that they want to maintain sole control. Most small business start-ups will not actually be able to gain equity funding, even if they wanted it, because providers of such capital are usually only interested in making a substantial investment. The normal criteria for most venture capitalists is a minimum equity investment of £250,000.

In some circumstances, however, especially where your own capital contribution is small and your borrowing requirement is large, equity funding will be essential as part of the overall package of funding. We have, of course, already looked at the gearing aspect in Chapter 2.

For the start-up business there are two likely sources of equity funding:

~ Business Angels

~ Regional Venture Capitalists

Business angels are private investors willing to take shares in a business. They may, or may not, take an active interest in the running of the business, although it is usual for them to have some expertise which the business can utilise.

The investment they make in your business is long-term and the actual terms of repayment can vary substantially. In some cases, no defined repayment programme is agreed, the business angel gaining a return on the investment by sharing directly in the profits.

The easiest way to find a business angel is to register with the National Business Angels Network. This organisation was established specifically to bring together businesses and private investors and it is sponsored by all the major banks.

Regional venture capitalists operate on a localised basis, offering smaller equity funding than the national venture capitalists. In some circumstances, the minimum investment that they will consider is £10,000, with a maximum investment of £250,000.

The investment is usually required in the form of redeemable preference shares with clearly defined terms on which they are to be redeemed. Time-scales can vary, but in general the investment will need to be paid back over a three- to seven-year period.

You also need to be aware that equity funding provided by a venture capitalist can be extremely expensive. The simple reason for this is that it is high risk lending and priced accordingly. It is not uncommon to see returns in excess of 20% per annum being required.

Obtaining equity funding can also be a long drawn-out process. You will need a comprehensive business plan, together with realistic and achievable financial forecasts for a three- to five-year period. Once your initial proposal is accepted, your business will then be subject to a process called 'due diligence'. This is an extremely thorough investigation of your business, usually carried out by expert professionals. *

* Gaining venture capital can be a painful process. It can take as long as three to six months from making the initial application to actually receiving the funding.

Summary points

★ Find out what assistance is available *before* you start your business.

★ Make any application for grants before you spend any money.

★ Contact your Local Authority and discuss your plans – you may be surprised at the help they provide to new businesses.

★ Visit your local Business Link to see what non-financial help may be available.

★ Do not dismiss equity funding – under the right circumstances it can be a critical part of your overall funding package.

Loan Repayment Tables

In order to help you establish the repayments necessary for any loan, two tables appear overleaf with various interest rates and repayment terms. In order to work out the monthly repayment for a loan you merely take the relevant cost from the table and multiply this figure by the amount of the loan that you require.

Please remember that these repayment tables can only provide a general guide to the repayments that will be required. The actual repayment amount will be based on when the interest is charged to the loan account. Some loans are charged interest monthly and others are charged quarterly. This is, of course, another aspect that you will need to consider when you are pricing the true cost of the loan.

As a specific example:

The repayment amount for a loan of £8,600 repayable over ten years at an interest rate of 12% is 8.6 x £14.35 = £123.41 per month.

Years	Interest Rates					
	10%	11%	12%	13%	14%	15%
1	£87.92	£88.38	£88.85	£89.32	£89.79	£90.26
2	£46.14	£46.61	£47.07	£47.54	£48.01	£48.49
3	£32.27	£32.74	£33.21	£33.69	£34.18	£34.67
4	£25.36	£25.85	£26.33	£26.83	£27.33	£27.83
5	£21.25	£21.74	£22.24	£22.75	£23.27	£23.79
6	£18.53	£19.03	£19.55	£20.07	£20.61	£21.15
7	£16.60	£17.12	£17.65	£18.19	£18.74	£19.30
8	£15.17	£15.71	£16.25	£16.81	£17.37	£17.95
9	£14.08	£14.63	£15.18	£15.75	£16.33	£16.92
10	£13.22	£13.78	£14.35	£14.93	£15.53	£16.13

Years	Interest Rates					
	16%	17%	18%	19%	20%	21%
1	£90.73	£91.20	£91.68	£92.16	£92.63	£93.11
2	£48.96	£49.44	£49.92	£50.41	£50.90	£51.39
3	£35.16	£35.65	£36.15	£36.66	£37.16	£37.68
4	£28.34	£28.86	£29.37	£29.90	£30.43	£30.97
5	£24.32	£24.85	£25.39	£25.94	£26.49	£27.05
6	£21.69	£22.25	£22.81	£23.38	£23.95	£24.54
7	£19.86	£20.44	£21.02	£21.61	£22.21	£22.81
8	£18.53	£19.12	£19.72	£20.33	£20.95	£21.58
9	£17.53	£18.14	£18.76	£19.39	£20.03	£20.67
10	£16.75	£17.38	£18.02	£18.67	£19.33	£19.99

Useful Contacts

British Chambers of Commerce
Manning House
22 Carlisle Place
London SW1P 1JA

Tel: (020) 7565 2000
Fax: (020) 7565 2049
www.britishchambers.org.uk

British Trade International
Department of Trade and Industry
Kingsgate House
66–74 Victoria Street
London SW1E 6SW

www.dti.gov.uk

British Venture Capital Association
Essex House
12–13 Essex Street
London WC2R 3AA

Tel: (020) 7240 3846
www.bvca.co.uk

Business Link Signpost Line
Tel: 0345 567765
www.businesslink.co.uk

Department of Trade and Industry
www.dti.gov.uk

National Business Angels Network
40–42 Cannon Street
London EC4N 6JJ

Tel: (020) 7329 4141
www.nationalbusangels.co.uk

National Federation of Enterprise Agencies
Trinity Gardens
9–11 Bromham Road
Bedford MK40 2UQ

Tel: 01234 354055

Small Business Service
www.businessadviceonline.org

Small Firms Loan Guarantee Scheme
www.businessadviceonline.org/SFLGS/

Small Firms Merit Award for Research and Technology (SMART)
www.businessadviceonline.org/SMART/

Phil Stone, Author and Management Consultant
Parkstone Management Consultancy
E-mail: help@pkstone.demon.co.uk
Website: http://www.pkstone.demon.co.uk
(Links to all of the websites above together with a large number of other useful sites can be obtained direct from this site.)

Further books written by Phil Stone

The Ultimate Business Plan

Buying a Franchise

Develop a Winning Marketing Plan

Accounting for the Small Business

Understanding Financial Accounts

Make Marketing Work For You

Financing a New Business